I HAVE SOMETHING TO SAY
ABOUT THIS BIG TROUBLE

I HAVE SOMETHING TO SAY ABOUT THIS BIG TROUBLE

Children of the Tenderloin Speak Out

With a Foreword by Dr. Maya Angelou

Collected by Reverend Cecil Williams and Janice Mirikitani

Glide Word Press
Glide Memorial United Methodist Church
San Francisco, California

This work contains poems, stories, and drawings used with the permission of the authors.

Notice to unlocated authors and artists:
This anthology contains the creative work of many current and former participants in the Mary Agatha Furth Children's Program at Glide Memorial United Methodist Church in San Francisco. The material was collected over the course of more than a year. Unfortunately, many of the children enjoy the program for only a few months before having to move on, and despite diligent attempts to locate each author and her or his parents, Glide Memorial Church has been unable to contact each and every contributor to this anthology for purposes of securing full consent to the use of her or his creative work. If your name appears as an author or artist herein, and you have not previously granted express consent to the use of your work in this book, Glide Memorial Church invites you to contact it at 330 Ellis Street, San Francisco, California, 94102.

Editor: Elizabeth Bluemle of Chalk Hill Press
Interior design: Armagh Cassil of SOMAR Graphics
Cover design: Veg Reisberg, using illustrations by Shawn Johnson, 8, and Tianah Maji, 9,
        of the Mary Agatha Furth Children's Program at Glide Memorial Church
Typesetting: Barbara Naiditch and Berna Alvarado of Metro Type

Publisher's Cataloging-in-Publication Data.
I have something to say about this big trouble: children of the tenderloin speak out.
ISBN 0-9622574-1-9 Softcover
1. Children's writings, American
2. American literature—California—San Francisco
3. American literature—20th century
4. San Francisco (Calif.)—Literary collections
I. Glide Memorial Church of San Francisco
Manufactured in the United States of America
10 9 8 7 6 5 4 3 2 1

Acknowledgments

Glide Word Press would like to thank the many people who have helped compile, organize, support and contribute to this project:

Furth Foundation, financial sponsor of the book;

Chalk Hill Press, provider of editorial, production, promotion and distribution arrangements, without financial compensation;

Peggy and Frederick P. Furth, benefactors of the Mary Agatha Furth Children's Program at Glide Memorial Church;

All the volunteers—tutors and recreational leaders, and the Boys' and Girls' Scout advisors—at the Children's Program;

Sandy Naylor, Tutoring Program Assistant;
Carl Leach, Teen Peer Tutor Advisor;

Advisory Board of the Children's Program:
Dr. Phyllis Kaplan, Dr. Kathy Perez, and Sylvia Walker; Joyce Hayes and Charlotte
        Quann, parents.

Special Thanks To:

Diana Johns, Preschool Program Director, and Lynn Bratcher, Parent/Child Community Outreach Coordinator, for collecting and keeping track of hundreds of poems, drawings and stories, and taking care of innumerable details under severe time pressures;

The mothers, fathers and extended families of the children for their support and care;

Richard Laurence and Lora Thielbar for their accounting and legal expertise;

Jean-Louis Brindamour, Carol Butterworth, The St. Vincent de Paul Society, and Daniel Vojir for having paved the way with similar projects and having graciously offered us the benefits of their experience;

Armagh Cassil, Metro Type, SOMAR Graphics, and Veg Reisberg—for being so accommodating, talented, and extremely knowledgeable about production;

Tiffany Bluemle, Chris Brown, Amanda Bay, Steve Rice, Norma Rodriguez, Christian Crumlish, and Katie Young for great ideas, unflagging enthusiasm, and boundless patience;

Dr. Maya Angelou for her powerful and inspiring words;

Terri Bush, June Jordan, Kenneth Koch, Nancy Larrick, Richard Lewis and Virginia Olsen Baron for their work in bringing children's voices to the attention of a larger audience.

Epigraph

In November, 1937, a million refugee children in Spain found themselves in emergency colonies set up by the government.

"When they first came to the colony, the children drew the things that were nearest and deepest to them—they drew planes and bursting bombs and houses in flames. You could see by the dreadful perfection of detail, how well they knew their subjects…"

—Dorothy Parker, "The Siege of Madrid"

Table of Contents

Preface

In 1981, with the launching of the Mary Agatha Furth Children's Program at Glide Memorial Church, Frederick P. Furth gave life to a vision that had remained close to him for many years. It was the vision of helping poor and homeless children raise the burdens of poverty and despair from their shoulders, burdens which had inhibited their growth, health and recovery, defaming their very images of themselves.

The program was created to provide a kind of intervention, so that children too long denied, ignored and set aside could fully realize their own potential. It was an investment of foresight and compassion, promising the most meaningful of rewards.

After all, in their own unique way, kids are the most creative, the most authentic, the most open among us, incredibly funny and incredibly wise. The kids at Glide are all of these things—and much more.

They come from the Tenderloin, a community in downtown San Francisco that is the most raw, the most painful, the most horrifying, the most poor, the most addicted, the most abusive. In the midst of all this *stuff,* the Children's Program is an oasis. And out of it comes life.

The program encourages these children to tell their stories in writing, on computers (through the newly established Computer Learning Center), in song, dance and art. With its one-on-one tutoring program in literacy, reading, math and other academic subjects, its preschool education and its motivational learning program, the Children's Program provides a foundation of basic skills.

(cont.)

With its special classes in drug abuse prevention and pregnancy prevention, and its peer tutoring program, the children's program offers an introduction to life skills so desperately needed.

The program also takes these children out of the concrete jungle of the community and into the experiential journey of museums, parks, aquariums, zoos, and amusement parks.

More than that, the children's program offers the children a safe place, one which nurtures and brings forth their dreams and opportunities.

In the grip of poverty and homelessness, Glide's kids are not without hope. Indeed, they have stories to tell. Here is part of their genius.

Reverend Cecil Williams
Janice Mirikitani

Tianah Awezi Maji, 9

Foreword

Where do children fit on the adult landscape? What hands do they have in the creation of an earth reeling with misery, weakened by hate?

They do not hurl explosives into the houses of the helpless. Rather, they inhabit those blazing infernos. Children do not poison the morning air with pollutants nor choke our rivers and streams with defecation, hospital waste, and chemical detritus. No, they simply breathe the air, drink the water and play upon the obscene beaches.

They did not invent the buying of souls nor the selling of dreams. Rather, too often, they themselves are the commodities sold and bought by their own community.

Children do not flood neighborhoods with crack and smack and cocaine, but rather their infant bodies are invaded with the fanatic drugs before they leave the wombs and struggle for their first breaths of air.

It is amazing that our children do not hate us, do not gather together as one strongly knit and righteously indignant group and turn their backs on us and this decrepit world we offer them.

This compilation of poetry, prose and drawings by children living on the ledge of life humbles me. I am humbled by the mysterious information in its contents: despite our society's malignant neglect, they the children, still reach their arms out searching for our love. Despite the many ways we have abandoned them, their poems still dance with hope for our acceptance.

(cont.)

Thanks to Reverend Cecil Williams, Janice Mirikitani, and the Mary Agatha Furth Children's Program, we are given another assurance that our crimes against the children can be erased if we will only act with love, and responsibility, and promptness.

Read this book. The children have already forgiven us, and while children may prevaricate, exaggerate, and fib, they do not lie. They must wait until we teach them that unhealthy action.

Dr. Maya Angelou
March 1989

Note to the Reader

The writings in this book have been edited as lightly as possible to retain the authors' freshness and style. Expletives, as well as misspellings which seemed to add to the meaning of a piece, remain as written.

Artist Unknown

Tila Paris, 9

Monster and the Magic Umbrella

One day Monster and the little boy got out of bed. The day was so hot. The sun was shining. So Monster said, "Come on, let's wash up and get dressed so we can go outside and play." So that's what they did. It was such a hot day. So Monster got his best hat and his umbrella to keep the sun off his face. Then everyone played ball. The sun was shining on them. They smelled sweaty.

Tianah Awezi Maji, 9

When I wake up I hear pigeons. Then I wipe my eyes and scare them. Do you want to know how I scare them? I hit the window because I don't like the sound they make. That's how I do. Then I hear the cars. They make terrible sounds. Then I close my window. I really don't like loud sounds.

Charmaine Broussard, 12

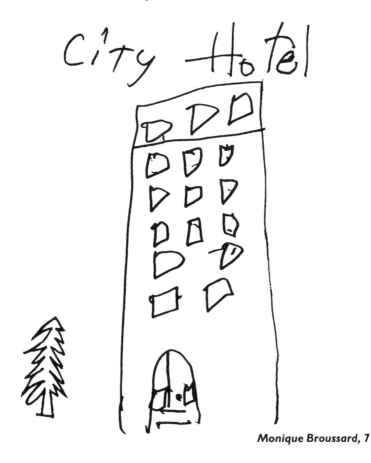

Monique Broussard, 7

It scares me to go alone and flush the toilet. And I'm scared of the dark and the big building because I afraid they are going to follow me. When I was two years old I was afraid that the sky will fall on me.

Lee Ferris, 8

Artist Unknown

Hello! My name is Neheshaa Pritchett, age 13 and in the 8th grade. I have 3 brothers and my mother. They are very, very nice people but sometimes they really work on my nerves. I attend Lowell Middle School in Oakland. It is a very good school to go to. I have a lot of friends who attend that school. I make good grades in school.

When I come home after school, I do my homework. I finish it and make sure the house is clean. Then I go over to my best friend's house. Her name is Shantel. We claim each other as sisters.

Well, when I grow up I want to be a lawyer or a beautician. Hair is one thing I can really do well. I will be thinking about some other things I might be interested in doing. I want to grow up and be somebody.

I thought I would just squeeze this in. My favorite people are my mother especially. My mother's friend and sometimes Joyce, my cousin Lucretia, Tauwaa, Danielle, and my grandmother. And my nerveracking brothers.

I think I am out of words to say. Bye, bye.

Neheshaa Pritchett, 13

1. I walk up the hill.
2. You walk down the hill.

Sandy Cu, 10

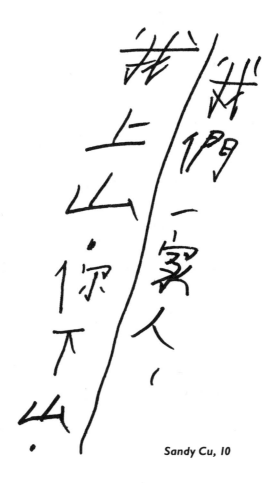

Sandy Cu, 10

R.J. Wroten, 13

Listen to this rap
It might sound like someone you know
Smoking that crack
And feeling kinda low

You destroy your mind
You have no pride
When a horrible feeling
Goes deep inside
You cannot hide

Just face the facts
'Cause you're a person addicted to crack
Always asking for money
From your mom and your pop
Soon as you get it
You go buy a rock

You tweaking on the fourteenth
You get paid on the fifteenth
Broke on the sixteenth
Children are starving having nothing to eat

Husband out there making the bread
But he don't know his wife is a hubba head
You need help and you need it bad
Before you lose everything you had
Your husband, kids, your mom and your dad

Selling everything that you ever own
Sometimes you act like you're in a twilight zone
You better quit smoking and stay alive
Before you really see the real dark side

Your kids see you smoking drugs
They don't need to see that, what they need is love

Henry Johnson, 14, and Randall Woodruff, 15

R.J. Wroten, 13

Boeddeker Park is great when they have special trips and activities like painting and tutoring. During the summer they have sports for girls and boys. But what would really make the park great is if there wasn't any bums or any other harmful people there. So far they have done a good job with keeping all the drunks out but they still need some more help. They should put more effort in keeping the big kids on their side and the little kids on theirs because too many kids get hurt that way. When they plan trips they should separate them like one for the little kids and one for the big kids. When a big kid want to have their party there they should be able to have it as long as they want but not too late and they should be able to have their own age group. Another thing is that when the kids go in the center they should be able to play the piano and run around. Well, I can't want everything in the world.

Shemika Skipworth, 12

Baron DeShay, 7

Dear Ronald Reagan:

Hi and how's the family. Well I'm not. I'm at home trying to figure out why you don't stop nuclear wars. People shouldn't have to think about Bombs and things like that. Maybe you should ask them how they feel. You don't have to ask me because I tell how I feel. I'm 13 years old almost 14 and I have something to say about this big trouble. Sometimes I sit back and think about Nuclear War and I get scared and sometimes I wonder what I would do. Ronald you have kids don't you? Ask your kids how they feel about Nuclear War and Nuclear Bombs. Here's something to think about. Stop Nuclear War! Think about all the babies that are in danger. Stop Nuclear War! Destroy all Bombs!

Have a very Merry Xmas.

Sincerely,

Winnie Oldy, 13

Tony Martinez, 10

My name is Sandy and I'm here to say
I wanna be an artist some kind way
I see some people who smoke crack
They might be an artist and that's a fact
But their dreams might never come true
Because of all the drugs they do
So don't do drugs, make your dreams come true
If you stay clean, there's nothing you can't do

Sandy Cu, 10

Shawn Johnson, 8

Dear Santa Claus,

This Christmas will you please make my grandmother a little nicer? And will you give me and my mother a new house please. Will you please give me a little kitten and a Barbie doll and a real baby, a sleepy real baby. I wonder if your house will be nice.

Will you feed the POOR PEOPLE.

Love,

Amber Evans, 10

Artist Unknown

God is a big man but what I think God look like he has a beard and has different colors like black, white, or any color. But I think God is everything around us.

Anonymous

Artist Unknown

Crack can kill
That's very ill
'Cause when you hit the hubba ya write ya own will
Don't think you're brave
'Cause the dope fiends crave
They pick you up
Throw you down in a park lonely brave
Don't come in my face
Just pick up ya pace
Ya going broke and ya know it if you get another lace
and
STOP THE BASE

Randall Woodruff, 15

Artist Unknown

Quyen Diep, II

34

Mother's Day

Hey, all mothers around the Bay!
You can't be sad on Mother's Day.

It's a time to listen, a time for hugs,
A time for kisses and a time for love.

A time to feed you breakfast in bed
And treat you like you got a crown on your head.

You always keep the house so clean
But today you don't have to 'cause you're the queen.

The best gift that I can give
Is to say no to drugs and decide to live.

Sugar is sweet and so are you;
This rap ain't finished until I say I love you.

Randall Woodruff, 15

My mother likes to talk about important things like our school report card, and like putting us in school. She talks to me and my sisters about different things that she doesn't want us to do. She also talks about what she's going to buy in the store. She talks about the news too. That's what's important.

Charmaine Broussard, 12

Shawn Johnson, 8

My mother likes to talk about mess. I don't know why but she do. The way it happens is when she finds out.

Anonymous

Tony Reed, 8

Good Luck

I would consider it
good luck if my
Mom had some
money.
10 million dollars.

She would buy clothes, shoes,
toys, a house, a new car, a new
couch, a new bedroom set. AND
I wish I had a toy house.

Edem Eyo, 5

Tianah Awezi Maji, 9

The mouse was looking for his mother. Then the cat came out, so the mouse ran. The sun came out, then the house turned yellow. The mouse came back, but the cat wasn't there, so the mouse went in the house. Then he was safe.

*   *   *

The mother mouse took a walk with the baby mouse. Then the sun came out. They went back home. When they got back home they took a good rest.

The End

Regina Smith, 7

Regina Smith, 7

Some Friends, Some Not

A friend is someone
you can trust,
not lie to you or treat you
like dust.
Some friends share
and buy you things
and they'll even
give up their golden rings.

I had a friend named Kira.
People tease her and
call her *mira*.

She is a good friend to me
you see.
We always talk of
what we want to be.

We talk, we play
everyday.
We spend lots of time together.

But here is someone
who acted like a friend.

There are kids who are wild and try
to take over me – yes, they try
to be better than me.
But I know that I am better.

I am on top
and I know it.

But God is my best friend.

Teneija Narcisse, 10

Artist Unknown

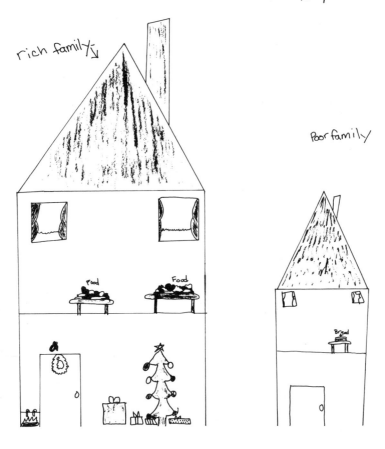

A happy Christmas
By Shemika Skipworth

rich family

Poor family

Shemika Skipworth, 12

A Happy Christmas

Once upon a time there was a very poor family and a very rich family. It was getting close to Christmas. The rich family had their Christmas tree and their presents all ready and the poor family had nothing but a single piece of bread. So one day the poor family went over to the rich family's house to ask for some food and all the rich family said was get away from my door. The poor family walked away sad. Well, it was Christmas Eve, everybody was happy except the poor family so that night the poor family went for a walk and the little girl stepped on an envelope. She picked it up and looked inside. There was $500 dollars. After that they had the biggest Christmas ever.

Shemika Skipworth, 12

Kids whose parents take crack:

The kids are mean.
Sometimes they steal candy from people.
I feel sad when they steal.
A lady with pipes and
stuff hit her baby for nothing.

Tisha Harvey, 8

Lawanna Bracy (age unknown)

Johnniemae Fairbanks, 13

When I am alone I see things and get scared and then I cover my face. Because I stay in a small room that's why I get scared. But when my mother comes I tell her about it and I don't get scared anymore. That's how I am.

Charmaine Broussard, 12

Lisa Ton, 11

The Greedy Girl

Once upon a time there was a girl who thought Christmas was every day. She was very greedy. Every day she wanted her mother or father to give her something. If they didn't give her anything she would scream she would kick and cry and jump on the couch with her shoes on. She wanted money, she always wanted to steal something, she wanted clothes, she wanted everything.

Tianah Awezi Maji, 9

Artist Unknown

Every day people walk down the street selling drugs.
People die one day at a time.
Some people.
Drug is bad for you.
Jail house. Peace. Love.

Regina Smith, 7

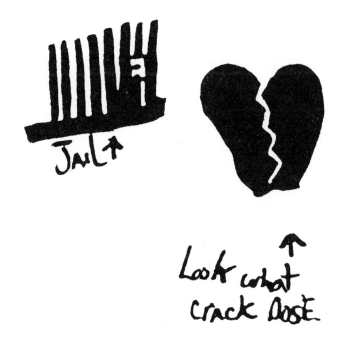

Artist Unknown

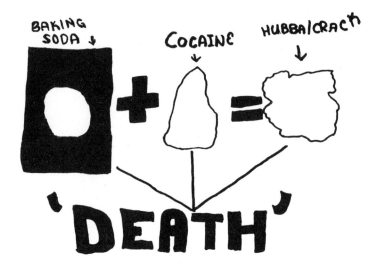

BAKING SODA ↓ + COCAINE ↓ = HUBBA/CRACK ↓

'DEATH'

Matt Dudley, 15

Baking soda, Miracle Whip jars
Fat donkey ropes, Mercedes cars

Beams on the ground, for drugs you're seekin'
You thinkin' you're cool but ya really tweakin'

Tweakin' so hard you sold your Caddy
And between your lips is a big fry daddy

I'm finished cappin', let's talk about me
I'm chill in a church called G-L-I-D-E

Smokin' that crack
Makes you look older

And for the rest of your life
You'll be lookin' over your shoulder

Listen up, Cecil and friend
My rap is over and this is the end

Randall Woodruff, 15

David Diep, 8

I like myself because I am a boy.
I like myself because I have black hair.
I like myself because I have brown eyes.
I like myself because I am myself.

Curtis Varner, 13

Artist Unknown

I like myself because I am a nice person to shy people. I like my friends. They like me because I am nice to them. My little brothers likes me too. My family likes me.

Tianah Awezi Maji, 9

a Wonder Family

Portia Bray, 8

To me my family
is best, It's better
than all of the rest.

Sometimes it's funny
when my dad calls
my mom honey.

Portia Bray, 8

Quyen Diep, 11

Martin Luther King was a great man. He helped black and white people. People liked Martin Luther King. One day he made a boycott. The boycott was the first one who gets on a bus gets to choose where they want to sit. And hired black people to be the bus drivers. They did the boycott over a year.

Tianah Awezi Maji, 9

Martin Luther King Birthday Celebration
January 15, 1989

On January 15th, people join hands,
not just from Mamphis but all over the land.
Martin Luther King was a very special man.
He joined black and white hand in hand.
The day he died was very sad
but his dream lives on and for that I'm glad.

You see, Martin Luther King was very good.
He marched and made speeches in every neighborhood.
He got beaten a lot but he stuck it out
and that's what the King was all about.
He wanted you to judge people without your eyes
and that led to the Nobel Peace Prize.

It doesn't matter what color your skin.
What matters is the love within.
King was a great man you can plainly see
and he proved his point because we are family.

He marched for freedom.
He marched for peace.
He marched for love
and for war to cease.

He fought for our rights
non-violently.
He went to jail
so we can be free.

So celebrate
Martin Luther King's birthday,
the man who earned us
our national holiday.

The Glide Kids

Peace

Artist Unknown

Susie Loc, 8

Once there was a girl name Rashaan. And she was a crack head. She lived in Potrero Hill projects. She had three kids and she was on welfare. Her kid's name was Keisha, Antonio and Tyeshia. Every time she got her check, she would spend it all on crack. And her kids were coming to school looking bummy and slummy. And everybody use to talk about them. They would always get into fights. Until one day. Rashaan got her check and she went to the back in the projects to get some crack. Then somebody hit her in the head and shot her in the mouth 3 times with a 357 at point blank range. It wasn't nothing strange because that's what happens when you buy crack.

Margaret Scott, 14, and Tina Robinson (age unknown)

Crack is bold.
Don't use it
or you'll die.

Alan (last name, age unknown)

Jesse Roberts, 9

Crack is a drug
It make you fall down
and go to sleep
When you wake up
you don't know nothing

Erica (last name, age unknown)

R.J. Wroten, 13

Facts on Crack

No one should take drugs because
it is not good for you. It's bad for you.
you can get hooked off of drugs. It may even
kill you, no matter how much you take.

Neheshaa Pritchett, 13

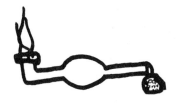

R.J. Wroten, 13

Christmas Day

The Holidays is
a time to care
a time for love
and a time to share

Hungry people
walk the streets
heads bowed down
feeling defeat

People over the world
feel love in their hearts
If you don't love now
why don't you start

Come to Glide
and get what they give
Don't be greedy
everybody has to live

Artist Unknown

The kids care
that's what we say
You should love all kids
any old way

The kids come to Glide
to get a hot meal
Cecilburgers and fries
that's a pretty good deal

So fill your hearts
with joy and cheer
Merry Christmas to you
and Happy New Year!

Randall Woodruff, 15

Artist Unknown

Hugs to you

Mom

Tila Paris, 9

My name is Jamar Pritchett. I attend the art school for now. But soon I will be going to Mac the school my brother goes to. I live in West Oakland with my family Truckee, Neheshaa, Tony and my loving mother Leester Pritchett. My mother is the bread winner in the house. She makes sure we have clothing, food and money for school, and I love her for that.

Jamar Pritchett, 15

I'm tellin' you
Stop crack before
we're through.

My mama said,
"You'd better go to school.
Get an education.
Be nobody's fool."

But I get bored
and wiggle in my seat
thinkin' about Fila jackets
and Adidas on my feet.

"Hey little dude,
wanna make some bread?
Just run these rocks and do what's said.
Do real good and you can have one.
Just kick back and have some fun."

I'm telling you
Stop crack before
we're through.

You look too smart
to be a dummy.
Crack ain't worth it
Don't care how much money.

If the rock man don't kill ya
then the rocks sure will.
With no kinda luck
you could go to jail.

You make the choice to live or die
So why, why choose crack
Crack get back
Stop the rock
Hubbas in troubba

I'm telling you
Stop crack before
we're through.

James Fairbanks, 11, and Johnnie Mae Fairbanks, 13

CRACK IS
TO YOUR BRAIN

Overton (Zip) Neal, 11

69

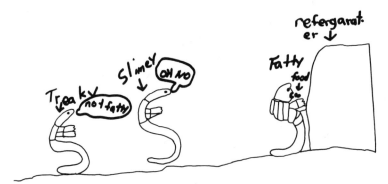

Tianah Awezi Maji, 9

The Three Snakes

Once upon a time there were three snakes. Their names were Slimey, Treaky, and Fatty. They all lived together. But they always fighted over things. One day Fatty was in the kitchen. You know he will eat up all the food. And all the food was gone! Fatty had ate all the Food! Fatty told Slimey and Treaky that all the food was gone. So that day they had told Fatty that they would buy a supermarket and they did. And they had food for the rest of their life.

I like to write notes and cards. I like to eat ice cream. My friends are nice to me, and I am nice to my friends. I love to ice skate. My birthday is on May 2nd. I am 9 years old.

Tianah Awezi Maji, 9

Artist Unknown

Holidays are fun because the grownups have fun on some holidays and the children would have some fun and children would have toys and candy and sometimes grownups can't have candy.

Teresa Hopkins, 7

Lisa Ton, 11

Tianah Awezi Maji, 9

Dear Ronald Reagan,

Why don't you stop buying "Nuclear War." Because it is destroying our city. Please stop spending our Welfare money on Nuclear Bombs. Do you know that we need that money to buy us some clothing and food. You should give some money to the poor and churches so they could feed us. This is what I really said at the beginning of my letter. Because I don't want you to feel hurt about what I said. Because I didn't mean to make you mad. I was just telling you that we need the money. I wish you a very happy merry Christmas.

Love always,

Patrice Denise Kelley Johnson (age unknown)

Artist Unknown

If you smoke crack
you are a "mac"
and I'm gonna tell you
some facts on that

Fact "1"
You go to the mail pick up your check
Go and smoke it up on a project step

Fact "2"
Now you're on the streets no where to go
You smoked up your check and you can't go home

Here's the end of the rap for me
but there's one last thing in my story

What I say I mean from my heart
The facts on crack is please DON'T START

Shemika Skipworth, 12

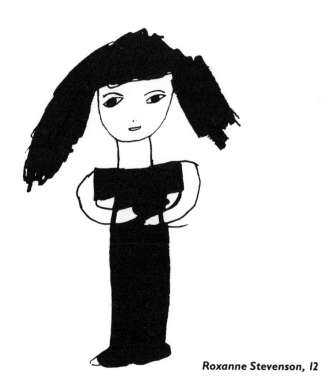

Roxanne Stevenson, 12

I have fun with my friend at home. I went with her one day to the movies. I went with her one day to the park. We went to her aunt. I like holidays too because I have fun.

Monique Broussard, 7

Artist Unknown

Three Stories I Like

The lion went outside to play. Then he heard a strange sound. So, he heard it again. Then he walked over to the bushes. It was two little worms.

*   *   *

One day there was a little boy. He saw a little girl walking to a pink and red house. She said "Hi" and he wanted to play with her. They went out to play. It was bedtime. Then they went to bed. The next morning they went outside to swim in the swimming pool. Then it got dark and they went to bed.

*   *   *

One time there was a little rat. He would make noise in the rat building.

Regina Smith, 7

Alonzo Thomas (age unknown)

Drugs are Dangerous

You buyem you smokin' em you're scandalous
The narcs got you spread against the wall

You had a Caddy, but now ya smoking
You tried to gaffel and you're choking on
A 38 you better set things straight
Or you will be lying dead center in a wooden crate

Now ya finished smokin' ya faced the facts
Then ya friend took you on to the tracks

You gotta rubber on ya arm and a needle in your hand
Then you start thinking if he's your friend
He shared the needle now he's getting laid
Now you gonna catch AIDS

I told you he wasn't your friend
Your lights are dimmin' that be the end

Randall Woodruff, 15

Ly Mui Chuong, 12

Miss Suzy Rich

Once upon a time there was a girl named Suzy. Her mother's name was Tina. She was eleven years old. She was very rich. She had lots of friends. One day when she went to school her friends ran to her. She had on a lace dress with big diamonds. Because today was picture day all the girls had on pretty dresses and the boys had on suits with bow ties so the girls would like them. Suzy was in 7th grade. She was the richest girl in school. After school she gave her friend Zizi 50 dollars. She always gave Zizi money because she is her best friend. They always go to each other's house. They always share stuff. They keep secrets from people, and they always share their lunch. One day when Suzy and Zizi went to school something terrible happened! Their school burned up. Zizi asked the fire fighter how long is it to fix the school back up? The fire fighter said it would take 12 months to fix it back up. Soon they fixed it back up. And Zizi and Suzy were still friends.

Tianah Awezi Maji, 9

Artist Unknown

86

If you use crack you will never come back.
If you take a drug you are a thug.
It makes you crazy and you become lazy.
That little pipe can ruin your life.
So be smart, don't start.

Aisha Brown, 10

People Make Me Angry When...

People make me angry when they steal my money.

Vinson Peterson, 9

People make me angry when they call me four eyed I don't like that and I want to slap people and hit them.

Anonymous

People make me angry when I go to this one place when you drive your car through a place like the zoo and you drive your car and there is all the things in the zoo.

Lee Ferris, 8

People make me angry when they do something bad to me all the time. When they act bad around me. When they tell on me when I didn't do it. They make me hate them.

Tianah Awezi Maji, 9

Artist Unknown

I think *crack* is like a *disease*, but like AIDS or herpes. It's like a *virus*. First it starts off cool when you smoke it a couple of times. Then when you start getting addicted it bothers your body. After that you probably start throwing up all over the place. Finally you will die.

R.J. Wroten, 13

Tila Paris, 9

Christmas is a Time

Christmas is a time when the family gets to gather and have a big dinner. Lots of love come into the family and all the people you dislike you love them. Christmas is a time when (Santa Claus) comes and gives good kids presents and the bad kids have to wait until next Christmas. Christmas is a time when you give presents and not expect them. Christmas is a time when you have parties at school at a friend's house and you have special treats like cookies, cakes, pies, candy and others. Christmas is a time when kids hang up their stocking, and expect a lot of goodies when they wake up.

Shemika Skipworth, 12

Artist Unknown

Once upon a time there was a little girl who lived on the edge of a big forest. One day when the little girl was walking through the forest she saw a dead rabbit, but it was not really dead. She screamed because she thought dead animals were gross, but when she screamed the rabbit woke up and spoke to her. The rabbit said, "I am sorry for scaring you. My name is Roger," said the rabbit. "You can speak English?" the little girl asked. "Of course you dummy." "Oh." "What's your name?" "My name is Latoya. Haven't you heard of me, you dumb rabbit!" "Oh. You must be Michael Jackson's sister and Janet's sister." "Well, I guess you rabbits must listen to records." "Yep, and we watch MTV, too," screeched the rabbit. Latoya said, "Didn't I see *you* in a movie recently? Didn't you play the rabbit in *Roger Rabbit?*" "I'm flattered that you recognize me. Do you want my autograph?" "Why would I want your autograph? I'm more famous than you. You should ask for *my* autograph!" "You singers are impossible!" said Roger, and he hopped off into the deepest part of the forest.

Tianah Awezi Maji, 9

My name is Ray
I'm here to say
Don't do crack
No how no way
It destroys your mind
It makes you stupid
Don't tell me
You already knew it

'Cause if you do
You blew it
Away like the smoke
Tomorrow you'll choke
The next day the next day the next day
You'll croak

If there wasn't crack, how would
We act? Brothers killing brothers
All the time
They start smoking crack
F—k the wine

If your friends are selling,
You better start yellin'
NO! I ain't stupid
Just because you did

Dope dealers gettin' shot,
Your friends don't care if you get popped
When you smoke it, it lifts you high
You start sayin' to yourself I could fly

You look in the mirror and what do you see
A Devil. Naw, that ain't me
Then your door rings who can it be
Flashing blue lights: S.F.P.D.

Walking down the street, who could it be
A old friend Joe, a roof job pro
459 on his car stereo. Alpine, Fisher, JVC's,
Motorola phones, Sony color T.V.'s
Had the car packed up to your head—
Freeze! flashing blue lights: S.F.P.D.

Now was it worth it, to go to jail
Or would you rather of went to hell
'Cause that's what you're doin', if you smokin'
I ain't jokin', and I'm hopin'
You'll remember my rhyme
Now go on your way
Have a nice day, hope you get what
I was tryin' to say

Ray Taylor, 15

Rayshea Caer (age unknown)

95

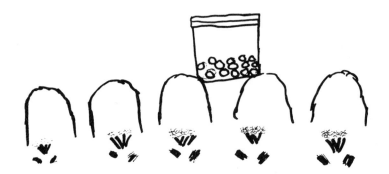

Ken (last name, age unknown)

Let me tell you something about CRACK
Don't even use it—turn your back.
You better stop it in this community
or you'll be shot to the curb for all eternity.

The rollers will catch the tweakers, you know.
The runners will have no place to go.

Do you know that you might die?
It will also make your children cry.

If you choose this mix
let me tell you now:
You got to stop
before it gets the babies down.

Tianah Awezi Maji, 9

Tianah Awezi Maji, 9

On a cold windy Halloween night, my friend and I were walking down a dark lonely road when out of no where a witch was in back of us and she was asking us all kind of questions and we wouldn't answer her. So she took us to her giant castle and she locked us up in one of her rooms. She had black cats and ghosts to watch us so we wouldn't try to get out. In the room there was also a round glass with sugar in it and it started going to the next part of the glass circle. The witch wanted us to try to get out before all of the sugar came out of the other part of the circle. It took us a long time to get out but we made it out and she told her ghosts and cats to try to catch us but we finally escaped from the castle and went where we were going and we never saw the witch again.

Neheshaa Pritchett, 13

Artist Unknown

100

Once upon a time there was a little girl named Tianah and she was on her way to school when suddenly she saw a man giving out balloons. When she went over to get one, she thought about what her mother Diana told her, not to stop on the way to school, but she still went over to get one. The man asked Tianah her name and she told him. He told her his name was B.G. and then Tianah asked could she have a balloon. The man said ok if she ride with him to get a bigger one she said I can't I have to go to school. The man said it would only take a few minutes and he would drop her off at school and she said okay. She hopped into the man's car and he drove off he took Tianah everywhere but to get a balloon and to school. Tianah started crying because she wanted to go to school and she wished she would have listened to her mother. Finally the man took her to school when she got there school was almost over. She went to the principal office Lynn when she went in she had butterflies in her stomach because Lynn was very mean. As she entered the principal asked what did you do this time Tianah said I'm sorry but this man asked me did I want to go with him and I did and he kidnapped me. Lynn said we'll talk about it later go to class. As Tianah went in to class her teacher Sandy asked why was she so late and Tianah said it was a long story.

Shemika Skipworth, 12

Crack is killer CRACK
is bad CRACK
Can destroy everythink you have.
Crack is a killer for your brain.
Crack can also make you die.

Roxanne Stevenson, 12

R.J. Wroten, 13

Crack is a bad drug that can make you step into your own grave. If you use crack, needles, coke, or pipes then you are just going to die. If a dealer is on a corner and ask you do you need some hubba just say NO! Crack is the most dangerous drug in the world. It is even more dangerous than cocaine. Crack will crack your head up. It will stop everythink and all you will want is that white rock. You see those people who are on the corner waiting for the dealers with their Mercedes and B.M.W.s and everything.

Truckee Pritchett, 11

Henry Johnson, 14

Artist Unknown

I want to talk about nuclear war
Innocent people died and live no more

We should learn from history
Let me tell you what it means to me
It could happen to any family

Hiroshima was a great civilization
They thought the war was over and then came the
    radiation
The kids were out in the street
When the bomb was dropped at their feet
They didn't know what hit them
They were burned by a great white heat

Their skin fell from their face
The heat so bad it was a disgrace
The pain so bad all over the place
What a sad day for the human race

This is the end of the rap from me
Let's get together for world and peace

Delashon (Shoney) Green, 10

My poem is about People

People are white, people are black,
People are yellow, people are red.
All these people no matter what color they are
Can do the same thing as the other one,
So all of these people should be friends to each other.

Jamar Pritchett, 15

Sandy Cu, 10

My name is Anthony Pritchett. I am 16 years old. I go to high school, and I am in the 11th grade. I live in Oakland in a household of 5 people, my two brothers and one sister and my mother. We all have a fairly good life.

Anthony Pritchett, 16

Sandy Cu, 10

Artist Unknown

At home with family is where love starts
Mom and Dad feel deeply in their hearts
Love is for me and love is for you
Love is for the world and people too
You can love your clothes and you can love your things
But there's nothing like love for human beings
Don't be mad don't be sad
Just open up your heart and be very glad
You have family on who you depend
You have your buddies you have your friends
When you talk about love
You feel it in your bones
If you want world peace
It starts at home.

Tianah Awezi Maji, 9

Ly Mui Chuong, 12

If I had magical powers on Halloween I would turn into a fairy godmother and give 3 wishes to all the boys and girls in the world who did something nice for someone or said something nice about someone. I would appear in a cloud of silver glitter and say, "You have done something nice so I will grant you three wishes." This would be fun because I would get to go all over the world to lots of different countries and I would be able to magically speak all the different languages. I would also get to be in more than one place at a time, like in Japan and Mexico. I would also go to Tahiti.

Linda Lynordowsky (age unknown)

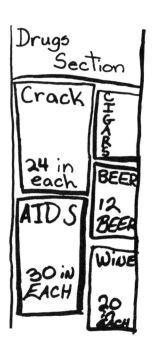

Artist Unknown

Crack is very bad for you.
It can kill you, yes it can.
If you do it
You might end up in a garbage can.
Please don't do crack, please, please, please.
If you stop I'll give you some cheese.
Please stop it before you die.
Stop now and I'll give you a pie.
Crack is not good.
Don't do it in your neighborhood.
THANK YOU BECAUSE YOU STOPPED!

Tianah Awezi Maji, 9

Shawn

Somebody smoking hubba.

SAY
NO
To
DRugs

Shawn Johnson, 8

Thinking you're hard
'cause you got the look
but behind the mask (but behind the mask)
you're just a rootie pootie

Don't come in my face
talking that junk
about who can beat who
and sound like a punk

I don't mess around
I don't go for crime
and if you're smoking crack
you're wasting your time

Don't wait till I turn my back
to talk trash
because you mad at me
because you don't have cash

You smoke so much crack
maaann that outraygus
Get the f— away from me
if you contagious

Randall Woodruff, 15

Crack is a Killer.
It can make you die.
It is bad for you.
You can get sick and die.
So just stop now.
Will people out there stop Crack
before you die?
I want you to not die
because I want you to live.

Tila Paris, 9

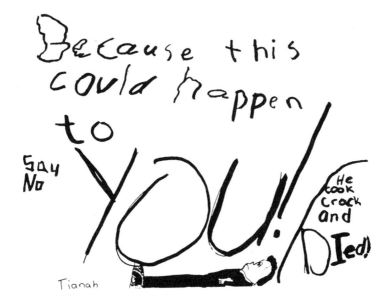

Tianah Awezi Maji, 9

My name is Shemika and I'm gonna rap
I'm gonna tell you how to learn math
Go to school and learn your numbers
Don't just sit at the desk and mumble
Go to Glide and get tutored
Maybe learn how to work computers
Learn subtraction learn your fractions
Learn addition and learn division
You might have competition
You might have to pay your tuition
Have faith don't debate
Return to school and be repaid
What I say is not a joke
This is for all you folks
Don't sit around or play around
Get a job then you can mob
My rap is ending but there's one last thing
Go to school don't be a fool
You know it

Shemika Skipworth, 12

Juneteenth Festival

They think black people sure are dumb.
Hey! young man, where're you from?

Listen up, people, this ain't no lie
It's about black people that fought and died
To get some freedom and not be slaves.
They fought to be free because they were brave.

In 1619 from Africa they came
Shackled, manacled and tied in chains.
Families and babies were torn apart
It hurt so much, deep in their hearts.
They were whipped and scolded, put to shame
They were tied up and thrown in flames.
Bought and sold on the auction block,
My black people—they hurt a lot.

How much you give me for this young male?
With good teeth and muscles like nails?
Or this strong wench
(We'll give her a pinch)
A fine breeder and a good housecleaner.

Worked the plantation
Blacks all over the nation
Stole their way to freedom
Fought slavemasters and beat 'em.

Thought they could break us
Put us to our knees
But we were moving, fighting to be free.

And now we're out and now we are free
We celebrate today —
June NINETEENTH!!!

I'm black and I'm proud
Say it out loud.

Randall Woodruff, 15

Tianah Awezi Maji, 9

Glide is a church and a community too
It offers love for me and you
It gives you hope and thrill of life
Makes you love your kids, your husband and wife
There's crack meetings for the needy
First Aid if they bleed
And if you're illiterate they'll teach you to read
They give the homeless food
They're never rude
And Cecil Williams is a real nice dude
This is what I wanted to say
I'm gonna say goodbye the Glide way:
I love you

Matt Dudley, 15

Artist Unknown

Dictionary of the Mix

This glossary of terms from the crack cocaine environment is included to help clarify words or phrases found in the book which may be unfamiliar to readers.

baking soda: used to cut down impurities of cocaine
base, basing: to smoke cocaine through a pipe
beams: see "highbeams"
capping: insulting someone sarcastically
chill: relax; relaxed
clean: drug-free
crack: cocaine in ready-to-smoke rock form
donkey rope: thick gold chain
fry daddy: a marijuana joint laced with crack
gaffel: fake rock cocaine; also, to sell fake rock cocaine
highbeams: the wide eyes of a person on crack (like car headlights)
hit: a rock that is being smoked
hubba(s): crack
hubba head: person addicted to crack
jars: containers used to mix cocaine with other substances
lace: to mix drugs with other substances
mac: a pimp
mission: to go out looking to buy crack
mix: 1) the cocaine environment; 2) whatever is happening to a person or persons in the cocaine environment
mob: to show off
narc: narcotics police
pipe: any object used to smoke crack
projects: public housing

(cont.)

rock: crack cocaine

rock house: place where crack is sold and/or smoked

rollers: the police

rootie pootie: a jerk

runners: people who transport dope for other people

shot: an amount of cocaine (i.e., 10 shot, 20 shot)

shot to the curb: lost everything to crack (financial destruction)

tweaking: to be in a state of drug-induced paranoia

Glide Memorial Church
Join the fastest growing volunteer force in San Francisco:
Call **(415) 771-6300**

Glide Church proudly offers:

Children's and Families' Program — Volunteers are needed to:
• tutor English, basic math, and writing skills
• counsel high risk kids
• teach cooking, sewing, and other classes in self-reliance
• assist children and parents in organizational skills
• teach personal hygiene and abuse prevention
• provide field trips for career opportunities
• supervise recreation and provide transportation.
(415) 771-4014.

Computer Learning Center — Glide needs:
• computer equipment and software
• cash donations
• lots of volunteers to train and teach.
(415) 771-4014.

Teen and Pre-Teen Program — Volunteers are needed to:
• coach teams
• counsel youth
• donate recreational equipment and video equipment
• be a big brother or sister.
(415) 771-6303.

Crack and Drug Addiction Recovery Programs — Glide needs:
• refreshments for meetings
• monetary contributions
• printing services for educational materials
• time and expertise in life support groups.
(415) 771-4014.

Mo's Kitchen at Glide — Serves 67,000 meals a month every month
for 365 days a year. (415) 771-6300.

Special Seasonal Programs — Volunteers are needed to:
• prepare food and serve meals
• organize canned goods production line
• stuff and distribute grocery bags of food
• wrap and distribute toys
• contact wholesale distributors and toy manufacturers
• organize pick-up and delivery systems
• handle telephone banks.
(415) 771-4014.

Order Form

Please make checks payable to: **GLIDE WORD PRESS**
Glide Memorial Church, 330 Ellis Street, San Francisco, CA 94102

All proceeds benefit the children's program at Glide Memorial Church in the San Francisco Tenderloin.

If you have friends who would like
I Have Something To Say About This Big Trouble:
Children of the Tenderloin Speak Out,
please let us send a copy or copies immediately, to:

Name: _____

Address: _____

_____

Quantity: _____ books at $9.95 each.   Total: _____

Californians please add $.65 sales tax.   _____

Shipping: $1 for the first book and
$.35 for each additional book, *or*   _____

I can't wait 3-4 weeks for Book Rate.
Here is $1.65 per book for First Class.   _____

Total amount enclosed: _____

I understand that I may return any book for a full refund if not satisfied.

Booksellers and Librarians: Orders may be made through
Publisher's Group West, 4065 Hollis, Emeryville, CA 94608.